Grade 2 Level 2 Elementary **Piano**

Improve your sight-reading!

Paul Harris

For online audio of all the pieces scan the QR code
or go to fabermusic.com/content/audio

FABER ✠✠ MUSIC

Practice chart

	Comments (from you, your teacher or parent)	Done!
Stage 1		
Stage 2		
Stage 3		
Stage 4		
Stage 5		
Stage 6		
Stage 7		
Stage 8		
Stage 9		

Teacher's name _____

Telephone _____

Many thanks to Jean Cockburn, Claire Dunham, Graeme Humphrey and Diana Jackson for their invaluable help, and particular thanks to Lesley Rutherford whose editorial skills and perpetual encouragement went far beyond the call of duty.

© 2008 by Faber Music Ltd.
This edition first published in 2018 by Faber Music Ltd.
Bloomsbury House, 74–77 Great Russell Street, London WC1B 3DA
Music setting by Graham Pike
Cover and page design by Susan Clarke
Printed in England by Caligraving Ltd
All rights reserved

ISBN10: 0-571-53302-7 (US edition 0-571-53312-4)
EAN13: 978-0-571-53302-2 (US edition 978-0-571-53312-1)

To buy Faber Music publications or to find out about the full range of titles available please contact your local music retailer or Faber Music sales enquiries:
Faber Music Ltd, Burnt Mill, Elizabeth Way, Harlow CM20 2HX
Tel: +44 (0) 1279 82 89 82 Fax: +44 (0) 1279 82 89 83
sales@fabermusic.com fabermusic.com

Introduction

Being a good sight-reader is so important and it needn't be difficult! If you work through this book carefully – always making sure that you really understand each exercise before you play it you'll never have problems learning new pieces or doing well at sight-reading in exams!

Using the workbook

1 Rhythmic exercises

Make sure you have grasped these fully before you go on to the melodic exercises: it is vital that you really know how the rhythms work. There are a number of ways to do the exercises – see *Improve your sight-reading* Grade 1 for more details.

2 Melodic exercises

These exercises use just the notes and rhythms for the Stage, and also give some help with fingering. If you want to sight-read fluently and accurately, get into the habit of working through each exercise in the following ways before you begin to play it:

- Make sure you understand the rhythm and counting. Clap the exercise through.
- Look at the shape of the tune, particularly the highest and lowest notes. Which finger do you need to start on to be able to play it? The exercises have this fingering added to get you started.
- Try to hear the piece through in your head. Always play the first note to help.

3 Prepared pieces

Work your way through the questions first, as these will help you to think about or 'prepare' the piece. Don't begin playing until you are pretty sure you know exactly how the piece goes.

4 Going solo!

It is now up to you to discover the clues in this series of practice pieces. Give yourself about a minute and do your best to understand the piece before you play. Check the rhythms and hand position, and try to hear the piece in your head. Always remember to feel the pulse and to keep going steadily once you've begun.

The **online audio** is for you to listen to *after* you have performed any sight-reading piece. Use it to check whether you have understood the rhythm and overall feel and style of the piece correctly.

Good luck and happy sight-reading!

Terminology:
Bar = measure

Stage 1

Reading right and left hands together is no more difficult than reading one hand at a time! It's like reading the following:

The	on	then	and
cat	the	saw a	had a
sat	mat	rat	chat!

No problem! The most important thing is *preparing very carefully* and *really understanding each piece* before playing it.

So, before you start to play, look carefully at the music and:
- Check that you understand the rhythm and counting.
- Know the key and play the scale and arpeggio.
- Know what notes you are going to play and which fingers you will use.
- Try to have a good idea of what it's going to sound like.

Rhythmic exercise

Write your own rhythm and then clap it:

Melodic exercises

Always count two bars in before you begin – one bar out loud and one bar in your head.

In the next three exercises notice that one hand repeats the same note.

Watch out for changing notes in both hands now! Play slowly and always *read ahead*.
(And remember to keep the pulse steady.)

Prepared pieces

1 What is the key of this piece? Play the scale (or microscale*) and arpeggio.

2 Play the first note in each hand and try to hear the piece in your head.
   In which hand is the melody?

3 What will you count? Tap the rhythm of the melody. Now hear that rhythm in your
   head and (at the same time) tap the rhythm of the right hand.

4 With which interval do both hands start?

5 Can you spot any repeated patterns – rhythmic or melodic?

6 How will you put character into this piece?

1 What is the key of this piece? Play the scale (or microscale*) and arpeggio.

2 In which hand is the melody? What pattern do the first three notes form?

3 What will you count? Tap the rhythm of the melody. Now hear that rhythm in your
   head and (at the same time) tap the rhythm of the left hand.

4 Play the first note in each hand and try to hear the piece in your head.

5 Can you spot any repeated patterns – rhythmic or melodic?

6 How will you put character into this piece?

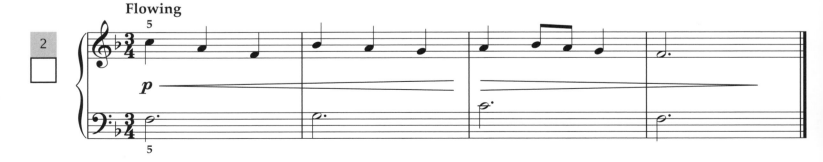

*See page 40 for details.

Going solo!

Don't forget to prepare each piece carefully before you play it.

Stage 2

More movement between the hands

More slurs and staccato

Rhythmic exercises

1

2

3

4

5

6 Make up your own rhythmic exercise:

Melodic exercises

1
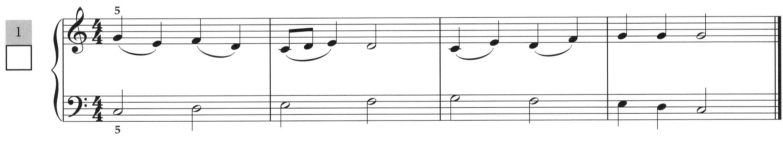

2
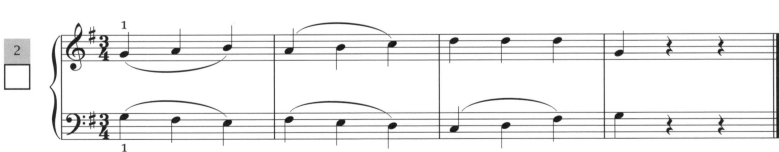

3

Prepared pieces

> **1** What is the key of this piece? Play the scale and arpeggio.
>
> **2** Which notes are affected by the key signature?
>
> **3** Can you spot any repeated patterns – rhythmic or melodic? Are there any scale patterns?
>
> **4** What will you count? Tap the rhythm of each hand separately.
>   Now tap the rhythms of both hands together.
>
> **5** Play the first note in each hand and try to hear the piece in your head.
>
> **6** How will you play expressively?

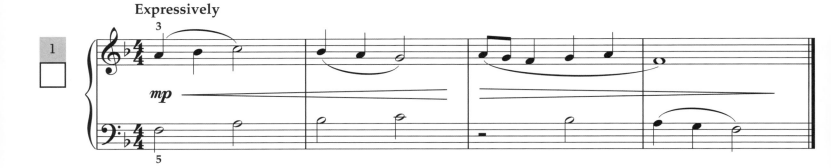

> **1** What is the key of this piece? Play the scale and arpeggio.
>
> **2** Only two notes are affected by the key signature – can you spot them?
>
> **3** What will you count? Tap the rhythm of each hand separately.
>   Now tap the rhythms of both hands together.
>
> **4** Can you spot any repeated patterns – rhythmic or melodic?
>
> **5** Play the first note in each hand and try to hear the piece in your head.
>
> **6** What ingredients will help you bring this piece to life?

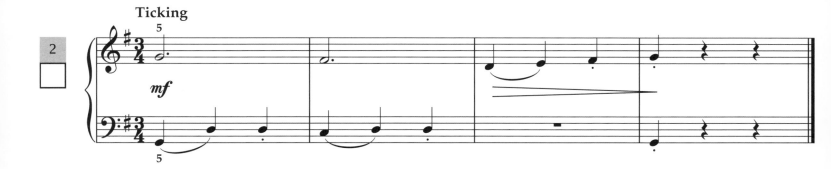

Going solo!

Stage 3

D major

Rhythmic exercises

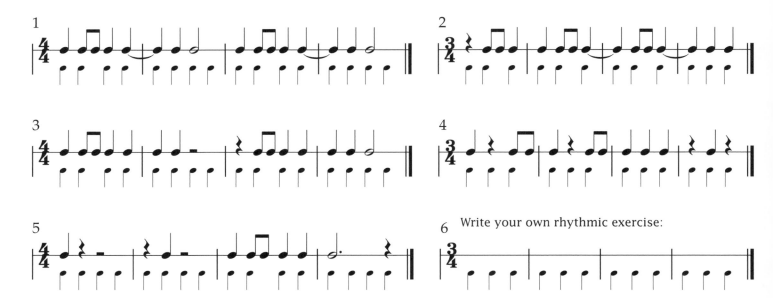

Melodic exercises

Play the scale and arpeggio of D major before you begin these exercises.

Prepared pieces

1 What is the key of this piece? Play the scale and arpeggio.

2 Does any part of the opening right-hand music return (in either hand)?

3 What will you count? Tap the rhythm of each hand separately.
Now tap the rhythms of both hands together.

4 What is the interval formed by the first two notes of the left hand?
Does this interval return anywhere?

5 Play the first note in each hand and try to hear the piece in your head.

6 What gives you clues to the character of this piece?

1 What is the key of this piece? Play the scale and arpeggio.

2 What pattern is the first bar in the right hand based on?

3 What will you count? Tap the rhythm of each hand separately.
Now tap the rhythms of both hands together.

4 Look for the lowest and highest notes in each hand and decide on your fingering yourself.

5 Study the left-hand part for a few seconds then try to play as much
as you can from memory.

6 What gives you clues to the character of this piece?

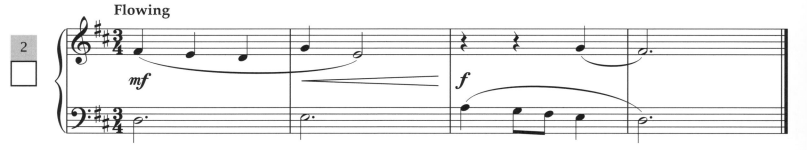

Going solo!

Don't forget to prepare each piece carefully before you play it.

Stage 4

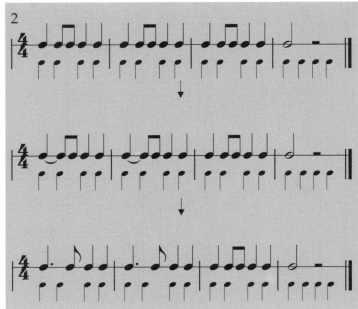

Rhythmic exercises

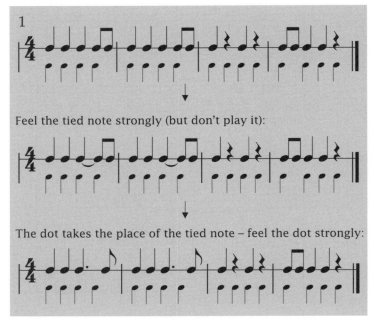

Melodic exercises

Prepared pieces

> **1** What is the key of this piece? Play the scale and arpeggio.
>
> **2** To which chord do the first three notes of the right hand belong?
> And the last three notes?
>
> **3** What will you count? Tap the rhythm of each hand separately.
> Now tap the rhythms of both hands together.
>
> **4** Play the first note in each hand and try to hear the piece in your head.
>
> **5** Study the first two bars of the right hand for a few moments then try to play them
> from memory.
>
> **6** What gives you clues to the character of this piece?

> **1** What is the key of this piece? Play the scale and arpeggio.
>
> **2** Find the three notes that are affected by the key signature.
>
> **3** Can you spot any repeated patterns – rhythmic or melodic?
>
> **4** What will you count? Tap the rhythm of each hand separately.
> Now tap the rhythms of both hands together.
>
> **5** Look for the lowest and highest notes in each hand and decide on your fingering yourself.
>
> **6** What gives you clues to the character of this piece?

Going solo!

In the next exercise notice the two different uses of dots!

Stage 5

♩. ♪ in 3/4

Rhythmic exercises

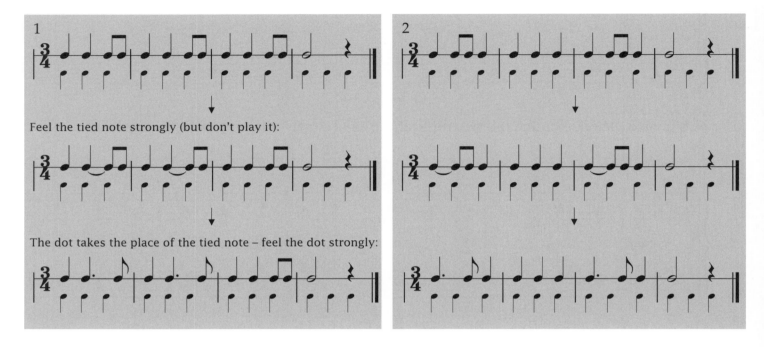

Feel the tied note strongly (but don't play it):

The dot takes the place of the tied note – feel the dot strongly:

Melodic exercises

Don't forget to look at the shape of the music and plan your fingering.

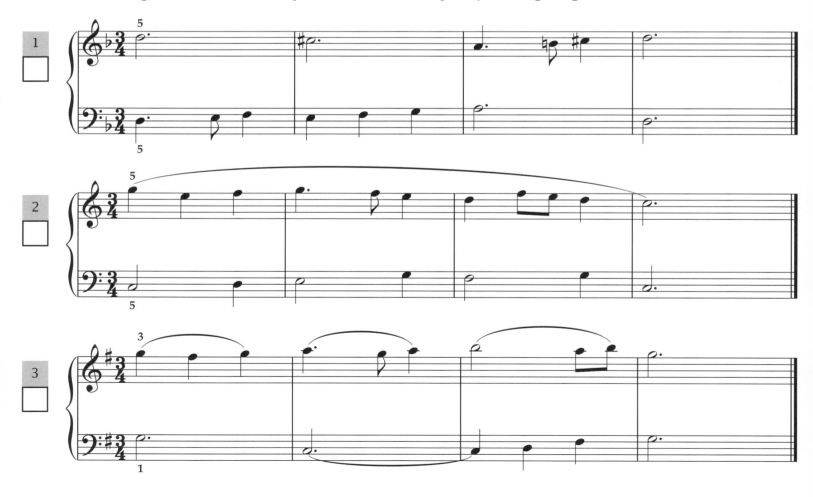

Prepared pieces

1 What is the key of this piece? Play the scale and arpeggio.

2 Which notes are affected by the key signature?

3 What pattern do the first three notes of the right hand belong to? Play that pattern.

4 What will you count? Tap the rhythm of each hand separately.
Now tap the rhythms of both hands together.

5 Play the first note in each hand and try to hear the music in your head.

6 What gives you clues to the character of this piece?

1 What is the key of this piece? Play the scale and arpeggio.

2 Can you spot any repeated patterns – rhythmic or melodic?

3 Can you spot any scale patterns?

4 What will you count? Tap the rhythm of each hand separately.
Now tap the rhythms of both hands together.

5 Play the first note in each hand and try to hear the music in your head.

6 What gives you clues to the character of this piece?

Going solo!

Don't forget to prepare each piece carefully before you play it.

Stage 6

E minor
More articulation

Rhythmic exercises

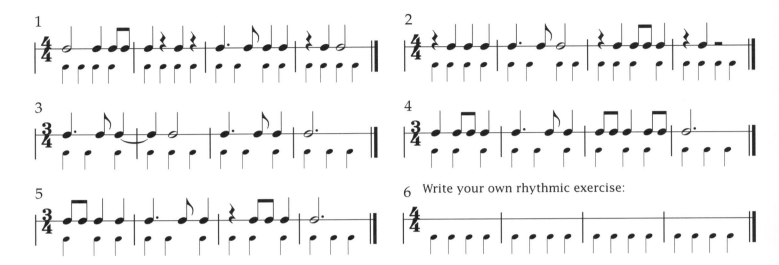

6 Write your own rhythmic exercise:

Melodic exercises

Play the scale and arpeggio of E minor before you begin these exercises.

Prepared pieces

1 What is the key of this piece? Play the scale and arpeggio.

2 Which notes are affected by the key signature?

3 What will you count? Tap the rhythm of each hand separately.
Now tap the rhythms of both hands together.

4 Can you spot any repeated patterns – rhythmic or melodic?

5 Play the first note in each hand and try to hear the piece in your head.

6 What gives you clues to the character of this piece?

Wistfully

1 What is the key of this piece? Play the scale and arpeggio. Look for the highest and
lowest notes in each hand and decide on your own fingering.

2 What gives the music its Egyptian flavour?

3 What will you count? Tap the rhythm of each hand separately.
Now tap the rhythms of both hands together.

4 Can you spot any repeated patterns – rhythmic or melodic?

5 Study the right hand for a few seconds then try to play as much
as you can from memory.

6 After you've played this piece make up your own Egyptian-sounding piece.

At the tomb of Tutankhamun

Going solo!

Stage 7

Rhythmic exercises

Melodic exercises

Play the scale and arpeggio of G minor before you begin these exercises.

Prepared pieces

1 What is the key of this piece? Play the scale and arpeggio.

2 What will you count? Tap the rhythm of the piece. Now hear the rhythm in your head.

3 What is interesting about the interval between the second and third notes (right hand)? Does this pattern occur again?

4 Can you spot any repeated patterns – rhythmic or melodic?

5 How will you put character into this piece?

6 Try to hear the piece in your head before you begin.

Dancing around the pyramids of Giza

1 What will you count? Tap the rhythm of the piece. Now hear the rhythm in your head.

2 What is the key of this piece? Play the scale.

3 How are the first two bars (right hand) related?

4 Can you describe the dynamic shape?

5 How will you put character into this piece?

6 Try to hear the piece in your head before you begin.

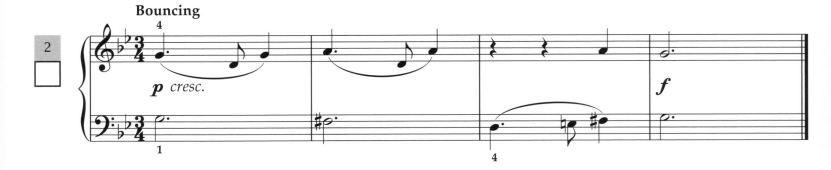

Bouncing

Going solo!

Don't forget to prepare each piece carefully before you play it.

Stage 8

Revision of keys

Rhythmic exercises

Melodic exercises

Prepared pieces

1 What is the key of this piece? Play the scale and arpeggio.

2 Can you spot any repeated patterns – rhythmic or melodic?

3 How many sections is this piece in? How can you tell?

4 What will you count? Tap the rhythm of each hand separately.
   Now tap the rhythms of both hands together.

5 How are the first and last two bars of the left hand related?

6 What gives you clues to the character of this piece?

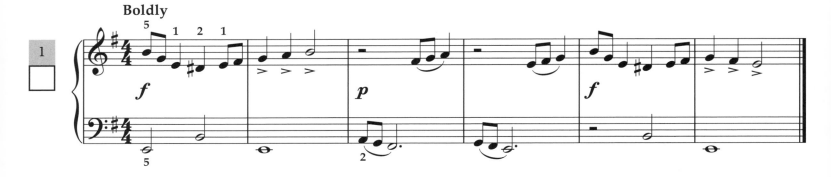

1 What is the key of this piece? Play the scale and arpeggio.

2 Which fingers will you use for the first note of each hand?

3 Can you spot any repeated patterns – rhythmic or melodic?

4 What similarities do you notice about the first and last bars?

5 What will you count? Tap the rhythm of each hand separately.
   Now tap the rhythms of both hands together.

6 How will you make this sound like a waltz?

Going solo!

Stage 9

Rhythmic exercises

Two golden rules

Always remember these two golden rules and your sight-reading will
go from strength to strength!
1 Don't begin until you're sure that you really *understand* the piece.
2 Once you've begun *keep the pulse steady* and *don't stop*.

Melodic exercises

Remember to count two bars before you begin each exercise –
one out loud and one silently.

Which of these pieces did you like best? Play it again and give it a title.

Prepared pieces

1 In which key is this piece? Play the scale.

2 Can you spot any repeated patterns – rhythmic or melodic?
  Can you spot a scale pattern?

3 What will you count? Tap the rhythm of each hand separately.
  Now tap the rhythms of both hands together.

4 What does the marking ♩ (bars 4 and 8) mean?

5 What does *cresc.* (bar 5) mean?

6 Find out what a rigadoon is.

1 In which key is this piece? Play the scale.

2 What do you notice about the first two bars?
  Study them for a few moments then try to play them from memory.

3 Can you spot an arpeggio pattern?

4 Can you spot any repeated rhythmic patterns?

5 What will you count? Tap the rhythm of each hand separately.
  Now tap the rhythms of both hands together.

6 What ingredients give you clues to the character of this piece?

Going solo!

The golden rules

A sight-reading checklist

Before you begin to play a piece at sight, always consider the following:

1 Look at the time signature and decide how you will count the piece.

2 Look at the key signature and find the notes which need raising or lowering.

3 Notice patterns – especially those based on scales and arpeggios.

4 Check the fingering and hand position for each hand.

5 Notice any markings that will help you convey the character.

6 Count at least two bars in.

When performing a sight-reading piece

1 Keep feeling the pulse.

2 Keep going at a steady tempo.

3 Ignore mistakes.

4 Look ahead – at least to the next note.

5 Keep your hands in position on the keyboard.

6 Play musically, always trying to convey the character of the music.

Look at each piece for about 30 seconds and try to feel that you are understanding what you see (just like reading these words).

Don't begin until you think you are going to play the piece accurately.

Microscales

If you don't know the whole scale, just the first five notes or even just the first three notes will do! Both patterns will give a good feel of the key.

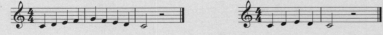